Baptism in the Holy Spirit

RANDY CLARK

For more information on how to order this book or any of the other materials that Global Awakening offers, please contact:

Global Awakening
1451 Clark Street
Mechanicsburg, PA 17055

1-866-AWAKENING

www.globalawakening.com

Global Awakening
{ Core Message Series }

It is our desire to bring the messages of the Kingdom to the people of God. We have taken what we consider to be core messages from Randy Clark's sermons and schools and printed some of them in booklet form. We hope this teaching increases your understanding of God's purposes for the times we are in and that you find yourself encouraged in your faith. Other core messages are available and they are listed at the end of this booklet.

Table of Contents

{ Introduction }

In the book of Joel, the prophet declares that a time will come when the Spirit will be poured out on all flesh (2:28-32). Hundreds of years later, Peter interprets the events of that first Pentecost as being the initiation of the fulfillment of that prophecy (Acts 2:14-21). And from that day forward, the church is now moving in a new dimension, empowered by the Spirit, having received the "promise of the Father". This experience of receiving empowering grace from God Himself, instead of being a powerful unifying factor bringing the church together as one family, has unfortunately at times been a source of division and strife, separating believers from their God intended destiny. The enemy has crept into the camp and caused many to think that various passages they read in Acts must be normative practice for the church, focusing on individual texts to prove their point, instead of seeing the overall picture of the Father's heart.

Rather than focusing on single passages as a framework, we should look at all the various ways in which Holy Spirit expressed Himself to the early church and see that God is very interested in bringing people into His family, using different experiences and forms to touch people with His love and grace. He doesn't seem interested in a particular order in which people experience them, just that they encounter His saving power and realize the fullness of Jesus' death and resurrection.

In this booklet, Randy re-examines some the controversy surrounding this important truth and teaches refreshing insights to help us have a more loving unifying perspective. God is committed to bringing down the walls that have separated us, both denominationally and individually. Sharing his understanding of these important biblical truths Randy reveals his heart for people to be equipped with understanding and with love that the Kingdom of God might bring transformation to people, churches and communities, that earth might become more like heaven, just as Jesus taught us to pray.

It is our prayer Lord for more of your Spirit to be poured out on us and through us to others, that your Name will be lifted up!

{ Chapter 1 }

Varying Views of the Baptism

There probably is no other experience within Christianity that has been more controversial than the subject of baptism in the Holy Spirit. At the same time, there is no other experience more important for a Christian than baptism in the Holy Spirit.

Christians have disagreed and been divided over when the baptism in the Holy Spirit takes place, what the initial evidence of the baptism is, and the process one goes through in receiving the experience of the baptism. I believe the Western mindset, which seems to need to systematize its doctrine, is part of the cause of this division. We like our doctrinal expressions to be neat and tidy, logical and consistent. We want to box God into our own doctrinal interpretation of the Bible. Therein lies the root of the problem with this division; God is greater than our doctrinal systems. Regardless of whether that system is Roman Catholic, Orthodox, Evangelical-Reformed, Lutheran, Baptist, Methodist, Holiness, Pentecostal, or Restoration Movement.

The above groups divide into four doctrinal systems in regard to the baptism in the Holy Spirit.

Infant Baptism

The Catholic, Orthodox, Anglican, Episcopal and Lutheran group believes one is baptized in the Holy Spirit at the time of infant baptism and that there is a renewed filling, or a stirring up of the gift of the Holy Spirit, which one receives at Confirmation.

At Conversion

The Evangelical, Reformed, Baptist, and Modern Methodist group believes one is baptized in the Holy Spirit at the time of conversion and there can be many subsequent fillings of the Holy Spirit.

Second Work of Grace

The third group, the Holiness groups like Church of God (Anderson), Nazarene, and others, believes that when one is born again of the Spirit, at that time they are indwelt and sealed by the Spirit. However, there is a "second definite work of grace" of the Holy Spirit, usually called "sanctification", which perfects one in love, gives victory over the carnal nature, and empowers the Christian.

Subsequent to Conversion

The fourth group (i.e., Pentecostals) has two subgroups. Both, however, see the baptism in the Holy Spirit as subsequent to conversion. They believe conversion is when one is born again, indwelt and sealed by the Holy Spirit. The baptism in the Holy Spirit must be sought and is subsequent to conversion. According to this fourth group it is not a simultaneous experience.

4

As mentioned, the Pentecostals basically divide into two subgroups. The first of the subgroups, with a holiness background, sees three stages in the Christian experience: (1) conversion, (2) sanctification, and (3) baptism in the Holy Spirit. The second subgroup, with a more Baptist background, has a two-stage view: (1) conversion, and (2) baptism in the Holy Spirit. Sanctification is seen as progressive. The Assemblies of God and the Apostolic Church are in this group (Bruner 1970, 92, 323-341).

When we come to the subject of the "initial evidence" of the baptism in the Holy Spirit, the Pentecostals, most Protestant Charismatics, and some Roman Catholic Charismatics say that "speaking in tongues" is *the* initial evidence of the baptism. Evangelical Christian denominations tend to emphasize the fruit of the Spirit, especially faith, hope, and love, as the evidence of the baptism in the Holy Spirit. The third group, the Holiness group, emphasizes the evidence of the "second definite work of grace" as being perfected in love, giving power to always resist temptation, and increased power to serve God and man.

As I consider the teaching pertaining to the baptism in the Holy Spirit, I shall not discuss at length the Catholic/ Sacramental understanding of the baptism in the Holy Spirit. Neither shall I consider at length the Holiness understanding. My emphasis will be to carefully consider the difference between the Evangelical perspective and the classical Pentecostal and most Protestant Charismatics' perspective.

It is my position that there is truth in each of these camps, but that each has tried to fit the witness of Scripture into its particular system. An additional position will be presented which is what I, and a growing number of other pastors, have come to believe better reflects the witness of Scripture. Some people call the position "Third Wave Theology", but, there is even diversity of opinion within this camp.

Finally, there are a growing number of people who hail from non-Charismatic, conservative Evangelical backgrounds but who have adopted certain classical Pentecostal practices such as healing the sick, casting out demons, and receiving prophetic revelations. Many of these people believe that the so-called baptism in the Holy Spirit happens at conversion and is not a second work of grace subsequent to the new birth. They also believe that tongues is simply one of many spiritual gifts and not the only evidence of a particular spiritual experience. Many of these people still see themselves as conservative Evangelicals, theologically and culturally, and have sought to relate their experiences of the Holy Spirit's power to conservative Evangelical beliefs (Nathan and Wilson 1995, 11).

{ Chapter 2 }

Definitions of the Baptism

An Evangelical Definition

My former professor at The Southern Baptist Theological Seminary, Dr. Lewis Drummond, gives the following definition of the baptism in the Holy Spirit. This definition is an extremely good representation of the Evangelical position, especially that of the Southern Baptists:

> This truth was first referred to by John the Baptist (Mt. 3:11). Then it was confirmed by our Lord (Acts 1:4,5) with reference to the initial enduement of the Spirit at Pentecost. Basically, it is the receiving of the Spirit by the believer (Acts 2:38; 1 Corinthians 12:13). It is analogous to "being made to drink into the one Spirit." **It is thus experienced by all true believers. It is also the act and experience whereby the believer is united with Christ and incorporated into the Body of Christ** (1 Cor. 12:12; Gal. 3:27,28). Further, it involves reception of power, since the Spirit is the powerful presence of God in us (Acts 1:5,8). It occurs at conversion to all believers (Drummond 1975, 78) (Emphasis mine).

A Pentecostal Definition

The following quotation is from the "Statement of Fundamental Truths" of the Assemblies of God, with which most Protestant and some Catholic Charismatics would agree:

> All believers are entitled to and should ardently expect and earnestly seek the promise of the Father, the Baptism in the Holy Ghost and fire, according to the command of our Lord Jesus Christ. This was the normal experience of all in the early Christian Church. With it comes the enduement of power for life and service, the bestowment of the gifts and their uses in the work of the ministry (Luke 24:49; Acts 1:4,8; 1 Corinthians 12:1-31.) **This experience is distinct from and subsequent to the experience of the new birth** (Acts 8:12-17; 10:44-46; 11:14-16; 15:7-9). With the Baptism in the Holy Ghost come such experiences as an overflowing fullness of the Spirit (John 7:37-39; Acts 4:8), a deepened reverence for God (Acts 2:43, Heb. 12:28), an intensified consecration to God and dedication to His work (Acts 2:42), and a more active love for Christ, His word, and the lost (Mk. 16:20) (Emphasis mine).

{ Chapter 3 }

The Evidence of the Baptism

> The baptism of believers in the Holy Ghost
> [in the Upper Room, on the day of Pentecost]
> **is witnessed by the initial physical sign of
> speaking with other tongues as the Spirit of
> God gives them utterance** (Acts 2:42). The
> speaking in tongues in this instance is the same
> in essence as the gift of tongues (1 Cor. 12:4-10,
> 28), but different in purpose and use (Menzies
> 1980, 388) (Emphasis mine).

Some Protestant Charismatics and most Roman Catholic
Charismatics would not regard tongues as the initial
evidence, but rather an evidence of the baptism of the Holy
Spirit. I personally believe it is possible to experience
the phenomenon of tongues without being baptized in the
Holy Spirit. Among this group, the baptism may occur
simultaneously with conversion or subsequent to conversion,
depending upon the individual's expectancy and other
criteria.

An important leader in the Roman Catholic Church, Cardinal
Leon Joseph Suenens, teaches that the baptism in the Holy
Spirit occurs at water baptism and is renewed at confirmation.

(For Catholic theology, the experience of regeneration/ conversion occurs at infant baptism.) He writes in his book, *A New Pentecost?*:

> Thus what many Catholics need to do is to realize that, for us, as well as the majority of Christian Churches, there is not a duality of baptisms, one in water and one in the Spirit. We believe there is but one baptism. Baptism in the Holy Spirit is not a sort of super-baptism, or a supplement to sacramental baptism which would then become the pivot of the Christian life....Our one and only baptism is at the same time both paschal and Pentecostal. To avoid from now on all ambiguity, it would be better not to speak of "baptism in the Holy Spirit" but to look for another expression....Different expressions are being used to define this experience of baptism in the Spirit: the grace of actualizing gifts already received, a release of the Spirit, a manifestation of baptism, a coming to life of the gift of the Spirit received at Confirmation, profound receptivity or docility to the Holy Spirit (Suenens 1975, 80-81).

Consideration of the Scriptures That Form the Basis of the Pentecostal Position

Acts 2:1-13	Pentecost
Acts 8:12-17	Samaria
Acts 9:1-19/ 22:16	Paul
Acts 10:44-46/11:14-16	Cornelius
Acts 19:1-9	Ephesian disciples

The above Scriptures are the primary ones used by Pentecostals in developing their view of the baptism in the Holy Spirit as an experience subsequent to conversion. They basically see all the personalities involved in the respective passages as already regenerated by the Holy Spirit, having entered into the New Covenant experience of the new birth.

The Evangelical understanding is that the above passages are descriptive of the new birth; which is the entry into the New Covenant at the time of Christian conversion. Simultaneously receiving the baptism in the Holy Spirit at conversion is understood to be the New Testament pattern. The Evangelical belief is the baptism in the Holy Spirit is an experience simultaneous with being born again.

While I was a student at the Southern Baptist Theological Seminary in Louisville, Kentucky, I met a graduate student, Larry Hart, working on his Ph.D. dissertation. His enthusiasm, love, joy, and Christian spirit really impressed me. We had several conversations while I was writing a term paper on the subject of the Charismatic Movement, and he was writing his Ph.D. dissertation on "A Critique of American Pentecostal Theology."

Larry, who is a Southern Baptist, shared with me that when he came to Southern Seminary he argued for the baptism in the Holy Spirit as a subsequent experience to conversion, just as any Assembly of God minister would do. He had received his BA degree in Psychology from Oral Roberts University, he later became Chaplain there and served as Associate Professor in the Religious Department at the University.

I was surprised when he stated he no longer believed the baptism in the Holy Spirit to be subsequent to conversion. Neither did he believe that tongues was the initial evidence of the baptism in the Holy Spirit even though he did have the gift of tongues. I asked him what changed his mind and he said, "The Bible." I asked what changed his mind about how he had been interpreting the Bible, and his answer was that he had read the book entitled "*Baptism in the Holy Spirit* by James D.G. Dunn." He came to his conclusions because he had been unable to refute Dr. Dunn's exposition of Scripture. I believe Dr. Dunn's book is still one of the most important books on this subject. It is a meticulous exegesis of all the biblical passages in the New Testament on this subject, and has also convinced me that the Pentecostal position demands that some Scriptures be given a meaning other than what appears to be the plain meaning of the context.

However, Howard Irwin's book *Conversion-Initiation and the Baptism in the Holy Spirit*, which was written to refute Dunn's book, has also convinced me that the Evangelical position demands that some Scriptures be given a meaning other than what appears to be the plain meaning of the context. This has brought me to the position that God is a God of diversity who does not have to fit his work into either the Pentecostal or the Evangelical position. He sometimes baptizes in the Holy Spirit at conversion, and at other times baptizes in the Holy Spirit subsequent to conversion. Sometimes tongues accompany this baptism and sometimes does not. I will now look at these Scriptures in more detail.

Acts 2:1-13

These verses describe the disciples' experience in the upper room. They were saints of God who were saved by faith, just as Abraham, Isaac, Jacob, David, and other justified believers in the Old Testament. However, they were unique because they lived in the interim time of the ministry of Jesus. The Holy Spirit was prominent in preparation for Jesus' ministry and upon those who shared in his ministry, but, like John the Baptist, they were still under the Old Covenant. The full experience of the Holy Spirit in an abiding manner was not possible until the New Covenant was established. This did not occur until the Day of Pentecost. Since today we do not live our lives in two dispensations or, in other words, under two covenants, the 120 disciples' experience cannot be the model for our Christian experience.

However, what are we to make of the eleven disciples who had received the Holy Spirit on the night of the first resurrection recorded in John 20:22? One cannot argue that Pentecost was their reception of the Spirit. For these eleven, the experience was subsequent. However, for the remainder of the 120, it appears to have been simultaneous with the regenerating work of the Spirit.

Acts 8:12-17

Acts 8:12 tells us that when the Samaritans "believed Philip as he preached the good news of the Kingdom of God and the name of Jesus Christ, they were baptized, both men and women." I want you to note they believed and were baptized.

Acts 8:14-17 tells us that the Apostles at Jerusalem sent Peter and John to Samaria when they heard that the Samaritans had "received the word of God." Peter and John "prayed for them that they might receive the Holy Spirit; for it had not yet fallen on any of them, but they had only been baptized in the name of the Lord Jesus. Then they laid their hands on them and they received the Holy Spirit" (vv. 15-17).

On the surface this passage does seem to teach, at least the possibility of, the baptism in the Holy Spirit being subsequent to conversion, but questions still remain. Was this experience, at the hands of the Apostles, their baptism in the Spirit subsequent to conversion or was it their genuine conversion with its correspondent simultaneous baptism in the Holy Spirit?

Dr. James D.G. Dunn believes the latter. He believes Luke means for us to understand that the Samaritans' faith was defective. He gives us two reasons for believing so. First, Luke does not use the usual Greek word for "believe" in reference to the Samaritans. Rather, he uses a different Greek word that means "to believe" (intellectual assent), which is head knowledge. It also means to agree intellectually with what has been said. Hence, intellectual assent to propositional truth is a defective belief because it does not involve the full commitment of the person. Secondly, Dunn believes that Luke intends to use Simon as a model for the Samaritans. Since Simon's faith was defective, so was the Samaritans'. (I find it interesting that this argument of Simon being a model indicating that the Samaritans' faith was defective is later not applied to Apollos and the Ephesian disciples. Consistency would demand that this model idea would prove the Ephesian disciples were really already Christian disciples like Apollos. Dunn, however, is not consistent in applying his arguments when they do not fit his system.)

Michael Green has noted that the word Luke used for "believe" is used for the saving kind of belief in other biblical passages and thus finds Dunn's argument weak. I, too, believe this is the weakest point in Dunn's book. Here, the Pentecostal perspective of subsequence is the most natural meaning of the text in its context.

I believe God, in His sovereignty, withheld the Holy Spirit in order to await the arrival of the Apostles from Jerusalem, in order that they might see first hand God's acceptance of non-Jews into the infant Church. This was the purpose of visible manifestations of the Holy Spirit, especially tongues, in the early days of the Church. It was a visible sign of God's breaking down prejudicial barriers and accepting all men and women into the church on the basis of repentance and faith alone. Though tongues were not specifically mentioned in this passage, some visible manifestation was present. The Bible explicitly says that "[w]hen Simon saw that the Spirit was given...." Some possible manifestations, which Simon might have witnessed are shaking, trembling, and being slain in the Spirit (cf., 8:18). I personally believe that if tongues were the primary manifestation, Luke would have stated so in the writing of the Book of Acts.

Acts 9:1-19; 22:16

Let us now consider the conversion of Saul of Tarsus who would later become the Apostle Paul. Pentecostals and many imprecise Evangelicals consider the experience of Saul on the Damascus Road to have been his conversion. But, this does not bear up under Scripture. Paul tells us in Acts 22:16 that after the Damascus Road experience, even after Ananias was used to heal his eyes, he told him to "rise and be baptized, and wash away your sins, calling on his name." In 9:17, Ananias tells Paul that God had sent him to Paul in order that Paul may regain his sight and be "filled with the Holy Spirit." Verse 18a tells us that "immediately something like scales fell from his eyes and he was baptized." Paul never tells us exactly when he was filled with the Holy Spirit. One can only conjecture. I believe, based upon Acts 2:38, that Paul probably received the filling of the Holy Spirit at the time of his repentance baptism, which was the New Testament means of expressing repentance and faith. His sins were forgiven at that time.

The main point is that Saul was not yet a Christian when Ananias came to him, so his filling with the Holy Spirit could have been simultaneous with his conversion as much as it could have been subsequent to his conversion. Scripture does not specify.

One last matter in Acts 9:5 to be considered is Saul's question, "Who are you, Lord?" He could not have been placing faith in Jesus with the title "Lord" because he did not know who was appearing to him. And further, the Greek word for Lord, "kurios" also had the meaning of "Sir". Saul was most likely using this latter meaning.

Acts 10:44-46; 11:14-16

Now let us look at the story of Cornelius. Pentecostals see Cornelius as already saved and the experience of tongues at Peter's preaching as his baptism in the Spirit, which was subsequent to his time of conversion. I do not agree.

It is true Cornelius was a religious man. He was "a devout man who feared God with all his household, gave alms liberally to the people, and prayed constantly to God" (Acts 10:2). Cornelius was a "God-fearer". This title was used for those Gentiles who embraced the moral law and worshipped the One God of Judaism. He too, was justified by faith under the Old Covenant. His experience, however, was not that of the new birth under the New Covenant.

Cornelius himself, told Peter that the angel had told him to "send to Joppa and bring Simon called Peter, he will

declare to you a message by which you **will be saved** ...”
(Acts 11:14). This clearly teaches that Cornelius and his
household received their conversion during Peter's visit and
his preaching to them.

Again tongues was given to verify to the Apostle Peter
the legitimacy of their conversion and acceptance by God.
Another barrier was torn down. Not only was God accepting
Jews and Samaritans, but now he was accepting Gentile
God-fearers into the Christian faith and Church.

This passage does not fit the Pentecostal system, just as
the Samaritan passage does not fit the Evangelical system.
Again, God does not fit His work into either the Pentecostal
or the Evangelical position on this subject. Rather, He is a
God of diversity that is revealed through both positions.

Acts 19:1-7

Finally, let us consider the case of the disciples at the city
of Ephesus. Again the Pentecostals find here a classic
text that seems to teach the baptism in the Holy Spirit as
an experience subsequent to conversion. They see these
disciples as Christians, but do not believe they received the
“baptism in the Holy Spirit.” This is based upon the King
James Version of Acts 19:2. It reads, “Have ye received
the Holy Ghost *since* ye believed?” Dunn emphasizes that
this is an inaccurate translation, which has been corrected in
the modern translations. The proper translation reads, “Did
you receive the Holy Spirit *when* you believed?” When I
first read Dunn's book, this argument convinced me, not
being a Greek scholar myself. Since that time, the New
International Version has been printed. In its footnote to
Acts 19:2 it has “after” as a possibility rather than “when.”

I realize now that the modern translations were completed since the beginning of the Pentecostal movement, and since almost all of the translators were not Pentecostal in their beliefs and experiences, that we have here a case of theology affecting translation when either "when" or "after" would be possibilities of reflecting the meaning of the Greek word.

I thought it would be very interesting to see how this verse was translated into other languages, as well as English prior to 1901. I found this so interesting that I called the library of The Southern Baptist Theological Seminary and asked them to send me the photocopies of English translations of this passage that would have been written prior to 1901. I received photocopies of four of the oldest English translations. They were written in the 1500s prior to the King James Version. All of them translated the word as "since" rather than "when."

Dunn believes Paul's question, "Did you receive the Holy Spirit when you believed?" really was a test to see if these men were Christians or not. The Apostolic preaching as recorded in Acts always mentioned the Holy Spirit; note Peter's Pentecostal sermon in the second chapter of Acts. How could these men have accepted the gospel of Jesus Christ and not have heard of the Holy Spirit? I believe it would have been very unlikely. Today's preaching, however, would find this omission of the Holy Spirit commonplace in much of the Church.

According to Acts 19:3-5, men had been baptized by John the Baptist but had not received Christian baptism. We know that Luke did not reserve the word "disciple" for Christian disciples only, for in his gospel he speaks of John the Baptist's disciples (Luke 7:18). Dunn believes they were the disciples of John the Baptist. They received the Holy Spirit at the time of their conversion, which was occasioned at the time of water baptism and Paul's laying on of hands. The tongues were present at the time of conversion-initiation and not subsequent to it. It should be taken into account that the term "conversion-initiation" allows for the concept of subsequence from a Pentecostal perspective because Pentecostals would not see baptism in water as necessary for conversion though it would certainly be a part of initiation into the local church.

It is not enough to hide behind the supposedly "correct" translation of Scripture and precise biblical language pertaining to the baptism in the Holy Spirit. Pentecostals and Charismatics today, like their spiritual forerunners of the Holiness Movement and the earliest Methodists, are to be praised for their emphasis on the experience of the Spirit.

I am presently reflecting upon my study in this area. As I do so, I recall Roman Catholic Cardinal Leon Joseph Suenens' language about "appropriating" the reality of our potential in Christ. Arnold Bittlinger, a German Lutheran Charismatic professor of Theology, believes:

> Every Christian has been baptized in both [water and spirit] or he or she is not a Christian in the full sense of the word. In baptism one receives potentially everything one will ever receive in Christ. But God's purpose in baptism must be actualized through the appropriation of its potential in the life of the individual Christian (Culpepper 1977, 59).

And again, from the non-Charismatic Southern Baptist professor, Dr. Robert Culpepper:

> It is better to speak incorrectly of a second blessing or a second Pentecost and lay hold of the reality of new life in Christ than to let the soundness of our doctrine rob us of its substance (Culpepper 1977, 72).

One of the great New Testament scholars of our day, Gordon Fee, has a wonderful chapter on the Baptism in the Holy Spirit in his book entitled *Gospel and Spirit: Issues in New Testament Hermeneutics.* Chapter 7, *"Baptism in the Holy Spirit: The Issue of Separability and Subsequence"*, is very helpful in healing the divide between Evangelicals and Pentecostals. Dr. Fee states:

> The purpose of this present essay is to open the question of separability and subsequence once again, and (1) to suggest that there is in fact very little biblical support for the traditional Pentecostal position on this matter, but (2) to argue further that this is of little consequence to the doctrine of the baptism in the Holy Spirit, either as to the validity of the experience itself or its articulation." (Fee 1991, 106-107).

He states again,

> "What I hope to show in the rest of this essay is that the Pentecostals are generally right on target biblically as to their *experience* of the Spirit. Their difficulties arose from the attempt to defend it biblically at the wrong point (Fee 1991, 108).

I find myself in total agreement with the position of Dr. Fee when he writes:

> In thus arguing, as a New Testament scholar, against some cherished Pentecostal interpretations, I have in no sense abandoned what is essential to Pentecostalism. I have only tried to point out some inherent flaws in some of our historic understanding of the texts. The essential matter, after all, is neither subsequence nor tongues, but the Spirit himself as a dynamic, empowering presence; and there seems to me to be little question that our way of initiation into that -- through an experience of Spirit baptism -- has biblical validity. Whether all *must* go that route seems to me to be more moot; but in any case, the Pentecostal experience itself can be defended on exegetical grounds as a thoroughly biblical phenomenon … **I think it is fair to note that if there is one thing that differentiates the early church from its twentieth-century counterpart it is the level of awareness and experience of the presence and power of the Holy Spirit.** Ask any number of people of today from all sectors of Christendom to define or describe Christian conversion or Christian life, **and the most noticeable feature of that definition would be its general lack of emphasis on the active, dynamic role of the Spirit.**

It is precisely the opposite in the New Testament. *The Spirit* is no mere addendum. Indeed, he is the *sine qua non*, **the essential ingredient, of Christian life.** Nor is he a mere datum of theology; rather, he is *experienced* as a powerful presence in their lives (Fee 1991, 110-111) (Italic emphasis Fee's, **bold emphasis mine**).

Dr. Fee sets out to indicate (by looking at the biblical texts to see reception of the Spirit as something that was part and parcel of their conversion experience) that this reception was inclusive of receiving the Spirit accompanied with visible manifestations of His presence.

> Indeed, it was the Pentecostals' ability to read the New Testament existence so correctly, along with their frustration over the less-than-adequate norm of anemia that they experienced in their own lives and in the church around them, that led to seeking for the New Testament experience in the first place. **The question, of course, is, if that was the norm, what happened to the church in the succeeding generations? It is in pursuit of that question that an understanding of the Pentecostal experience as separate and subsequent lies** (Fee 1991, 116).

Dr. Fee raises the questions whether or not the Pentecostal experience must be seen as not biblical because it does not fit the biblical pattern, or if they need to reinterpret the Bible to fit their experience. To both these questions he answers NO! **How then are we to let the Bible speak clearly what it says, and also validate the Pentecostals' experience of the Spirit?** He writes:

> On the one hand, the typical evangelical or reformed exegete who disallows a separate and subsequent experience simply must hide his or

her head in the sand, ostrichlike, to deny the reality–the biblical reality–of what has happened to so many Christians. On the other hand, the Pentecostal must be wary of reforming the biblical data to fit his or her own experience. The solution, it seems to me, lies in two areas: (1) An examination of the components of Christian conversion as they emerge in the New Testament, and (2) an analysis of what happened to Christian experience once the church entered into a second and third generation of believers.

Without belaboring any of the points in detail, it seems to me that the components of Christian conversion that emerge from the New Testament data are five:

1. The actual conviction of sin, with the consequent drawing of the individual to Christ. This, all agree, is the prior work of the Holy Spirit that leads to conversion.
2. The application of the atonement in the person's life, including the forgiveness of the past, the canceling of the debt of sin. I would tend to put repentance here as a part of the response to the prior grace of God, which is also effected by the Spirit.
3. The regenerating work of the Holy Spirit that gives new birth, that brings forth the new creation.
4. The empowerment for life, with openness to gifts and the miraculous, plus obedience to mission. This is the component that

Pentecostals want to make *subsequent* to numbers *1, 2, 3,* and the Protestant tradition wants to limit simply to fruit and growth, but tends at times seemingly to omit altogether.

5. The believer's response to all this is baptism in water, the offering of oneself back to God for life and service in his new age community, the church. This act obviously carries with it the rich symbolism of elements 2 and 3 (forgiveness and regeneration), but in itself effects neither.

The crucial item in all of this for the early church was the work of the Spirit; and element 4, the dynamic empowering dimension with gifts, miracles, and evangelism (along with fruit and growth), was normal part of their expectation and experience. (Fee 1991, 117-118)

Fee points out that the problem is that point 4, the dynamic reality of the Spirit became lost in the subsequent history of the church. A condition arose which was very different from the experiences of the New Testament believers.

Christian life came to consist of conversion without empowering, baptism without obedience, and grace without love. Indeed the whole Calvinist-Arminian debate is predicated on this reality, that people can be in the church, but evidence little or nothing of the work of the Spirit in their lives (Fee 1991, 118).

Few would argue that this is the case, but how did this situation develop?

There are two main reasons for this development. The first is that the New Testament was written to first generation Christians who were baptized as adults, thus the issue of second and third generations wasn't addressed. The conversions for the succeeding generations of those who grew up in Christian homes would not be so dramatic or life changing. The dynamic experiential nature of the conversion experience would be the first to go. (Fee 1991, 118)

The second reason, and most devastating, was the connection between water baptism and the reception of the Spirit. With the eventual acceptance of the practice of infant baptism the dynamic experiential nature of conversion was lost. This would prove to be the case for most of Christian history, but it was not the situation in the Bible. All the pietistic movements since the Montanists to the Toronto Blessing must be understood as a reaction to the sub-normal life of the Christians in the church in comparison to the life in the Spirit that is depicted in the Bible (Fee 1991, 119).

It is precisely out of such a background that one is to understand the Pentecostal movement with its deep dissatisfaction with life in Christ without life in the Spirit and their subsequent experience of a mighty baptism in the Spirit. If their timing was off as far as the biblical norm was concerned, their experience itself was not. What they were recapturing for the church was the empowering dimension of life in the Spirit as the normal Christian life.

That this experience was for them usually a separate experience in the Holy Spirit and subsequent to their conversion is in itself probably irrelevant. Given their place in the history of the church, how else might it have happened? Thus the Pentecostal should probably not make a virtue out of necessity. At the same time, neither should others deny the validity of such experience on biblical grounds, unless, as some do, they wish to deny the reality of such an empowering dimension of life in the Spirit altogether. **But such a denial, I would argue, is actually an exegeting *not* of the biblical texts but of one's own experience in this later point in church history and a making of that experience normative.** I for one like the biblical norm better; at this point the Pentecostals have the New Testament clearly on their side (Fee 1991, 119) (Italic emphasis Fee's, bold emphasis mine).

The above quotes can be summarized as follows; the Pentecostals view of the Baptism in the Holy Spirit to be the evidence of speaking in tongues at a subsequent experience to their conversion, is based upon weak biblical support. The Evangelicals have done an even greater injustice to the biblical text by almost totally missing the nature of Christian life as a life of vibrant, dynamic, supernatural life in the Holy Spirit. The necessity for a subsequent experience is the Spirit is not necessitated by biblical texts but rather their place in Christian history, because for many people their baptism in the Spirt was subsequent.

I believe Evangelicals owe a great debt to the Pentecostals. They, along with the Charismatic Movement that followed later, have been virtually alone in emphasizing that the charismata, grace gifts, are still the birthright of the Church. They rejected dispensationalism's view that the gifts of the

Spirit were dying out with either the death of the Apostles or the canonization of the New Testament.

Today, many within the Evangelical camp are listening to their brother Pentecostals and Charismatics brothers. We cannot deny the genuine accounts of the "sign gifts" in operation today. The Charismatics particularly have left the "saw-dust" trail and have entered the graduate departments of our universities. Much of what they say about the gifts is well balanced and biblical. It is actually more accurate than Evangelical interpretations of the gifts. What I am excited about today is the possibility of Evangelicals being open to expecting and experiencing the gifts of the Holy Spirit while not having to identify with the Pentecostal interpretation of the "baptism in the Holy Spirit"; nor what I believe has been a legalistic-Pharisaic attitude within much of Pentecostalism. We must, as God does, look at the motive behind this legalism within Pentecostalism. I believe it is motivated by a misunderstanding of Christ's understanding of holiness coupled with a deep love for Him. Therefore, let us be temperate in our condemnation of this legalism. In reality, this legalism seems to be passing away, and it must also be noted that there was also legalism on the part of many Evangelical groups at the turn of the century.

Furthermore, let us not forget the multiple examples of great men and women of God who spoke of an experience, call it what you may, subsequent to conversion which radically changed their lives and made them victorious: men like John Wesley, D.L. Moody, R. A. Torrey, and Charles Finney.

I personally sense my inadequacy in the area of ministry and relationship to the Holy Spirit. David (Paul) Yonggi Cho and the late John Wimber have emphasized our need to be intimate with the Holy Spirit. Mike Bickle calls this "developing a secret history with God." This is the deep need of the Church today.

{ Chapter 4 }

Appropriating the Baptism

I have given much thought to the prerequisite conditions for this spiritual experience of the baptism in the Holy Spirit, if there are any conditions. It seems to me that the first possible condition is to become aware of our personal inadequacy in our Christian life. We must recognize our defeatedness, our indifference, our lack of power, and lack of faith, etc. Second, we must desire for this condition to change. By this I mean we develop a serious desire or hunger to be victorious Christians. Third, we must want our lives to honor God and to be used in his service, for his glory. Then, we do not ask for a spiritual high to make us feel good, or for an experience that can boost our ego or spiritual pride. Rather, we are asking for power and gifts to make us commensurate to the task before us of binding the "Strong Man" and plundering his home. The task is that of "breaking down the gates of hell." For in our victory God is glorified, honored, pleased, and we are edified. This empowering enables our faith to express itself in love.

Billy Graham said:

> I think it is a waste of time for us Christians to look for power we do not intend to use: for might

in prayer, unless we pray; for strength to testify, without witnessing; for power unto holiness, without attempting to live a holy life; for grace to suffer, unless we take up the cross; for power in service, unless we serve. Someone has said, "God gives dying grace only to the dying" (Graham 1978, 107).

I am excited about what I see happening in the body of Christ right now. Since I went to Toronto Airport Vineyard and was used to begin the meetings, I have been privileged by God's grace to meet key leaders of both Evangelical and Pentecostal streams. I am discovering there is much more openness to diversity of spiritual experiences than there was twenty years ago. I find Pentecostals open to working with me, knowing that I don't believe one must speak in tongues to be baptized in the Spirit; though I have had a prayer language since 1971 yet it did not occasion my baptism in the Holy Spirit. At the same time, I am finding Evangelicals who are open to working with me knowing that I do believe in the gifts of the Spirit, and in the baptism of the Spirit occurring both simultaneously with conversion, and more often subsequent to conversion. I am finding men of Evangelical stripe who admit they were baptized in the Holy Spirit after their conversion; I am also meeting Pentecostals who admit that they believe one could be baptized in the Holy Spirit before receiving one's prayer language, at the time one received it, or after one received it.

In summary, the traditional walls are beginning to fall. Why? Because desperation has risen in the hearts of people to experience what the Bible speaks of in such experiential terms, rather than being satisfied with a tidy, supposedly theologically correct understanding of the baptism in the Spirit.

While I was attending seminary at the Southern Baptist Theological Seminary in Louisville, Kentucky, I was told by Dr. Louis Drummond about the great Shantung Revival among the North China Mission of the Southern Baptist Convention. Although I graduated in 1977, I had never read anything about the Shantung Revival (the book I reprinted in 1995) twenty years later. For several weeks I had an impression coming into my head to get anything written about the Shantung Revival and read it. I was captivated by this revival among Southern Baptist missionaries in 1932. It is clear it began among the leadership who were tired and burned out. They admitted their need for more and discovered that some of the leaders among them were not even truly born again. The emphasis was a study of the Bible relating to the Holy Spirit and a baptism of the Holy Spirit. As I read Shantung Revival I found everything that has been happening in the Toronto Blessing, except the animal sounds, which have been so blown out of proportion. I write this April 18, 1996, and to the best of my knowledge there have only been 12 times that there were animal sounds at the Toronto Airport Christian Fellowship, and only three times in meetings which I have led. Considering there have been meetings six nights a week since January 20, 1994, in Toronto, and I have been in over 350 Renewal meetings, 15 occurances is not indicative that this is one of the main things God has been doing in this Renewal.

But, about the other things that often occur -- the shaking, the falling, the crying, the laughing -- all of these things occurred in the Shantung Revival. These things seem to occur everywhere people have been seeking the fullness of the Holy Spirit. I have found evidence of this in Protestant revivals from all over the world, from Roman Catholic histories of revival, and from the Bible.

RANDY CLARK

{ Chapter 5 }

Summary

Let me state that I believe the Bible does not fit either the Pentecostal or the Evangelical systems regarding the baptism in the Holy Spirit, both are too narrow. I believe the same God that did not make two fingerprints or two snowflakes alike did not intend to make our experience of his Spirit to be the same for everyone. When we look back at the passages in Acts we find that the people were baptized in the Holy Spirit at a prayer meeting with tongues (Acts 2) and at another prayer meeting without tongues (Acts 4:31). Sometimes the Spirit came after baptism with the laying on of hands, with no tongues occurring (Acts 8). At other times, we are not told the particulars of how or when someone was baptized with the Spirit (Acts 9). Baptism in the Spirit can occur at the time of conversion, before water baptism, with tongues and prophecy accompanying it (Acts 10). Or it can also occur after water baptism with the laying on of hands accompanied by tongues and prophecy. There does appear to be at work here a God who likes diversity, and I suggest we need to learn to like diversity. I believe if we could learn to appreciate this biblical diversity, it would enable us to appreciate the diversity within the body of Christ, which Satan has used to divide us.

In my church we honor and welcome people who have had experiences reflecting this New Testament diversity. We do not try to convince them that their experience is not valid, or is not normative. Rather, we emphasize that God is free to baptize us and fill us with his Spirit in whatever way he so chooses. In this manner we can find unity in the midst of diversity.

As a matter of fact my emphasis has not been so much on the experience of being baptized in the Spirit as it has been on the fruit of having an intimate relationship with Jesus Christ. The reason I have encouraged the people of my church not to ask someone if they have been baptized in the Spirit is that the answer doesn't really tell one much. What do I mean by this? Well, it's like asking someone if they have had a wedding. They may answer, "Yes," but you don't know anything about the relationship. They may be living in hell in the marriage or in marital bliss. They may have had a wedding, but are now divorced, widowed, or separated. One does not really know much about the relationship by asking someone if they have had a wedding. Rather ask them about how intimate they are with their mate and if they love him/ her more today than when they first married.

In like manner, people could have had an experience, call it baptism in the Holy Spirit, years ago but now they are cold, lukewarm, or backslidden, or they may be passionately in love with God. Focus on the relationship. In this way people cannot hide behind an experience of the past. It is not enough to have had a baptism in the Holy Spirit; we must continue to be filled with the Holy Spirit.

Not only does the Bible reflect diversity of experiences pertaining to the baptism of the Holy Spirit, but also the history of the Church does. I must believe that Jesus was right when he made the evidence of the Holy Spirit to be the reception of power (Luke 24:49 and Acts 1:8). I believe Arthur Blesset was right when he told us we should emphasize the "red," referring to the words of Jesus in the Bible. When I read the history of the Church I find men who had received power and then had a powerful influence upon the Church and society. Some of these people, like Francis of Assisi, Ignatius Loyola, and Mother Teresa, were Roman Catholic; others like George Whitefield and Billy Graham were/are Reformed; others like John Wesley, E. Stanley Jones, and Charles Finney were Arminians; and still others like Maria Woodworth-Etter, John G. Lake, Smith Wigglesworth, T.L. Osborn, Oral Roberts, Omar Cabrera, Carlos Annacondia, Claudio Freidzon, Luis Palau, and David Yonggi Cho are Pentecostals. I cannot believe that the non-Pentecostals mentioned above were not baptized with the Holy Spirit because they did not speak in tongues, and that others who have spoken in tongues, but who have had little impact upon the Church and society have been baptized in the Spirit. If power is a major purpose and evidence of the baptism in the Holy Spirit, then I must acknowledge both Church history and the Bible indicate that people can be baptized in the Holy Spirit with diverse experiences in how they received this baptism. See the book, *Powerlines*, which records the expressions of the Spirit in many famous Evangelicals.

Billy Graham concludes his book, *The Holy Spirit* with this illustration:

> Over 100 years ago, two young men were talking in Ireland. One said, "The world has yet to see what God will do with a man fully consecrated to Him." The other man meditated on that thought

for weeks. It so gripped him that one day he exclaimed, "By the Holy Spirit in me I'll be that man." Historians now say that he touched two continents for Christ. His name was Dwight L. Moody. (Graham 1978, 220)

Let us strive to be spiritual leaders of the Church, willing to pay the price of putting His Kingdom before our own. May we desire to have many repeated fillings of the Spirit in order that we might be known as men and women full of the Holy Spirit. Let us humble ourselves before God that he might lift us up. Let us truly acknowledge our personal weakness that we might turn from self and the flesh to Christ and the power of his Spirit. Let us love one another as mutual leaders in his Church and pray for each other, confess our sins to each other and carry each other's burdens. Let us quit fighting each other and fight the real enemy, Satan, who accuses the brethren.

{ Chapter 6 }

Case Studies of Baptisms

A personal baptism in the Holy Spirit
Randy Clark, Pastor of the Vineyard, St. Louis,
Missouri. October 27, 1989 10:45 a.m.
Last night was the most powerful experience of God's presence to date. It was more powerful than my conversion as far as experiencing the manifest presence of God. (I am not talking about the experience of grace-forgiveness at conversion). It was more powerful than the experience I had at the 1984 James Robison Bible Conference--an experience of great humbling, love, and emotion. It was more powerful than the "baptism in the Holy Spirit" which occurred in March 1984 that lasted for 13 minutes and was characterized by electrical power running through my body. This fresh baptism was awesome because God alone is awesome.

I am writing this down because I never did record the other experiences, believing at the time I could never forget any of the details. However, time and experience have proven otherwise. I do not remember clearly the details of those experiences with God. I do know, however, that those above mentioned experiences, and my healing and being called to preach, have altered the course of my life and its purpose. They have been radical experiences producing radical changes in my life.

I now shall try to put into words -- which cannot adequately describe the glory of the experience -- my reflections on last night's meeting, and my fresh baptism in the Holy Spirit.

The meeting was the seventh session of the 1989 Regional meeting for the Association of Vineyard Churches. I went not really expecting some new empowering, but rather some better understanding of the many changes the Holy Spirit was initiating in the Vineyard movement. The six previous meetings had been good, but I had sensed no stirring by the Holy Spirit in regard to myself. The last meeting was Thursday night and Todd Hunter spoke on "Obedience." Near the end of the message I felt the Holy Spirit beginning to affect me. Hot tears were running down my face. They were not tears of conviction, but tears of confirmation--of God's nearness, and of God's heart for evangelism. (Todd was alluding to evangelism at this point in his message.) At this time I had a strong impression that of the five-fold ministry, evangelism /evangelist was what I was called to do. I had been struggling with this issue for some time. John Wimber had told me that he felt God had shown him twice that there was an apostolic call upon my life. That was in 1985 and in 1986. He had told me the first time we met and he prayed for me (January 1984), "You are a Prince in the Kingdom of God...." and other encouraging prophetic words.

Bob Jones had told me in August of 1985 that I had a strong "teaching anointing." Only the day before this experience, Bob Jones said I was anointed in revelatory gifts-prophecy, in evangelism, and in pastoring. However, I felt like all this was too vague.

While I was sitting, listening to Todd, with tears running down my face, I had the strong impression: "You're for evangelism—you have always loved leading people to the Lord and preaching evangelistically." I thought, " I will go forward during ministry time and ask God to confirm this call to evangelism, or anointing for evangelism." I thought somebody would speak prophetically to me as confirmation. The invitation was for those pastors who sensed emptiness in ministry, a lack of power and anointing, and who realized a lack of power in praying for the sick. When I went forward, Happy Leman came and prayed for me. I do not remember exactly what he said, but he said nothing about evangelism. Another person came to pray for me; I do not know who she was. Both times I sensed a low-grade anointing of the Holy Spirit, but nothing really powerful or confirming happened.

I then felt impressed to have Steve Nicholson pray for me. I had prayed for him in August of 1985 and there was a prophetic insight to pray for "all the gifts commensurate to the office of an apostle." God came, and Steve was consumed by the Holy Spirit. Now I felt he should pray for me. So, I asked him to pray for me and he did. He prayed for the restoration of vision and faith in me, and for the restoration of expectancy and power like I had known in '85 after a long fast. He prayed for God's purposes to be renewed in me. He said, "You thought you could just pastor one congregation in St. Louis, but God has more in mind," and other things which I do not remember.

The anointing of God resting on me grew more powerful and it became difficult to keep standing. The power in my hands, especially the right hand, intensified to about a 6 on a scale of 0 to 10, with 0 equal to no witness and 10 equal to painful witness of power or electricity. My hands were shaking from the electricity. However, Steve said nothing about "evangelism" to me. After he finished praying I kept standing at the altar area because I still felt God's presence and power resting on me. About ten minutes later the benediction was given but I had resolved not to open my eyes or move from where I was standing as long as I felt God's presence on my physical body. Finally the witness became so weak that I opened my eyes, and turned around to prepare to leave.

A very brief period of time passed when Ron Allen, the Area Pastoral Coordinator in Indiana came up to me. He asked where DeAnne was and how my son was doing. I answered Josh was fine. Then he said, "The enemy has tried to take your son, but he did not succeed. Joshua and you will stand hand in hand before the nations." I was still so dazed that I made what I now know was an inadequate response. I just smiled and said, "That's good."

Ron left and I sat down to write what he had just told me. When I did, the reality of what he said hit me and I began to weep. I knew Ron was especially gifted in evangelism. I thought, "I'll tell him what I believed God had impressed upon me about being for evangelism." I was thinking that, like Timothy, I would be connected with a local church as a pastor and primarily be engaged as an evangelist within the pastoral role.

I went up to Ron and told him all of this. He did the Bob Jones "thing" of hand to hand, and said he felt the witness of the middle finger--representing evangelism. He felt that what I was sensing was true. I did not put much confidence in the hand to hand "thing" of Bob Jones, so this did not convince me. Ron then asked me if he could pray for me.

I believe what happened this time in prayer was God's confirmation of His earlier impression. When Ron began to pray, immediately there was a witness of strong anointing on Ron. The hand he put on my chest was shaking and I could feel electricity going from his hand into my chest -- about a 3 on the scale. My right hand began to feel electricity, which caused it to twitch and then shake. As he continued to pray, I began to feel electricity in my left hand, but without the twitching or shaking. It was "buzzing."

I was standing there with my eyes closed and overheard Ron tell someone to blow on my heart. When the person did I was "slain in the Spirit." It was as if I had been pushed down, but nobody pushed me in the slightest way. Right before this happened, the power in my hands had reached a 7. When I fell to the floor everything intensified and I was now really affected emotionally, not just crying but weeping loudly and uncontrollably. I felt what I believe was God's heart and His love for me. I was praying quietly, "Thank You God, Thank You God," and was repenting for having lost vision, expectancy, power, and love for Him and His purposes. I was overwhelmed by the sovereignty of the event and its intensity. Then the power began to get stronger and I felt it intensify from 7 to 9 in both hands, and it was now becoming uncomfortable and even painful. I remember crying, "Oh God! Oh God! Oh God!" As the power continued to intensify, I remember responding with groans and ouches. My hands had become contorted, my fingers extended out with the first joints from the fingertips pointed downward and the middle joints locked. I could not unlock my fingers' positions. I was shaking my hands due to the discomfort in them. Then my fingers began to be drawn down toward the palms. The index fingers felt separated and pulled towards the thumbs and there was considerable discomfort in my hands. Simultaneously, my face felt like electrical power was coursing through it, almost like some lace fabric that had been energized was laid on my face. It was as if an electrical mask had been applied to my face and was not only drawing electricity as it was drying, but was also emitting electricity. There was a weight upon my chest that felt like my chest was in an electric vise grip.

Then, I felt my arms being pulled above my head and my body being stretched. The current became so strong in my hands that I lost all feeling of my hands above the wrists. I had electricity running through my body and I felt as if I was lying on my side with my feet cramping. (The sensations seemed to intensify when Ron would pray things pertaining to evangelism.)

Finally, all the intense electricy gradually began leaving and normal sensations returned to my hands. My rapid breathing started slowing down. I had been blowing, like a woman in labor who was using the Lamaze method. The heat, which I experienced, that had caused sweat to run down my face, also left.

I was aware of everything happening to me and around me. I felt very weak, almost dazed. I know I had been a sobbing spectacle to the crowd, but I could not help it. Through the whole experience there had been no fear, but rather an awesome sense of the power, glory, and love of God. (If I had never heard or seen similar experiences I probably would have been very frightened by it.) In the natural, this would have been a most humiliating experience, but in the Spirit it had been encouraging and intimate. What C. S. Lewis wrote is true. Lewis said of the lion that is the Christ figure in his *Chronicles of Narnia*, "Aslan is not a tame lion."

Finally, I got the courage to open my eyes. Robert Stovall and someone else helped me off the floor. I was weak and somewhat drunk (i.e., staggering and disoriented). After a couple of minutes I could walk without help. I had to hold my hands up because if I let them down to my side they would "buzz" (feelings of electricity) so strongly that it was very uncomfortable.

What did all this mean? Was it the confirmation I was looking for? Were the prophecies really of God? I do not know what it all means, yet I am grateful for the experience. I do believe it was God's confirmation for giving myself to evangelism in my church and beyond.

The above was written the morning after the experience. Weeks later I realized I had experienced a deliverance during this experience. It has been eleven years now (Dec. 2000) and I have continued to walk in victory (over a specific sin) that, prior to this experience, seldom lasted eleven weeks.

Steve Stewart - Pastor of Cambridge Vineyard, Ontario, Canada - March 16, 1994

On Monday, Jan. 24th, in response to an invitation by John Arnott, I attended one of the meetings led by Randy Clark. Although I saw a number of people obviously impacted by the Holy Spirit (i.e., laughing, crying, falling, shaking, etc.), I felt very much an observer throughout the evening and did not go forward to receive prayer myself. A week later John Arnott again urged me to come attend another one of the meetings, and so on Tues. Feb. 1st I did so, accompanied by all of our pastoral staff. During the worship three of my children went up to the front to be with John and Carol Arnott and the Spirit of God fell upon the two youngest.

John and Carol beckoned my wife and me to the front where we found two of our children on the floor laughing and seemingly unable to get up while another of my sons prayed over both of them. A few minutes later, Randy invited all of the pastors and their wives to receive prayer in an adjoining meeting room. My wife and I gathered along with our staff and approximately 50 other people. When I was prayed for, I felt the presence of the Lord come and rest upon me, albeit somewhat gently, and I rather quietly slumped to the ground. A few minutes later I got up and to my surprise discovered almost all of our staff stretched out on the floor. As I stood there looking at them, John Arnott came over and, aware that he had a very sore throat, I offered to pray for him. Almost as soon as I laid my hands on him and began to pray, the power of God hit both of us and we both fell almost violently to the ground. Observers later said we looked like two bowling pins flying through the air. As soon as I hit the ground the power of God fell upon me in a way I've never known before and I began to laugh loudly and uncontrollably. This continued for several minutes, and then I found myself beginning to weep and feel extremely powerful muscle contractions around my middle. Frankly, it felt like what I imagine birth pains to be. For the next couple of hours I laughed and cried. I was also aware that I was having a great deal of trouble speaking. I stammered almost uncontrollably and often I would 'lock up' on a single word. I also began to fall over again and again. Almost invariably, once I felt that I was under control and could get up and walk, as soon as I tried to take some steps I would fall over again. This probably happened somewhere between twelve and twenty times. After some time I began to pray for other pastors and leaders, and the power of God fell on many of them. Around 1:00 a.m. some of the staff helped me out of the building and into our van. Needless to say, someone else drove!

This began what has been a most remarkable journey for me. Over the past six weeks the power of God has not only fallen on me again and again, often without any warning whatsoever, and often not even in the context of any meeting, but as well, I have prayed for hundreds and hundreds of people and seen the Holy Spirit fall upon a very high percentage of them. I have just returned from Russia where, without me telling them anything about what has been going on in our own church, when I prayed for people, manifestations took place in Russia identical to those which took place here. People in Russia fell over, shook, laughed, and cried. There has been a significant amount of demonic manifestation as well. An interesting aspect of this though, is that the demonic spirits leave almost immediately upon being addressed. We have been holding meetings for many weeks now in the Cambridge Vineyard, and have seen countless hundreds touched by God.

John 15:26 and 1 John 5:7 both state that the Holy Spirit testifies to Jesus Christ. I would say that one of the most significant results of this move of God has been that we have experienced the common testimony of many that the presence and person of Jesus Christ have become so much more real. We certainly have seen more people come to Christ in the last six weeks than at any other six-week period in our history. This renewal has touched our small groups, children's ministry, Junior High teens and young adults' ministry. As a church we find ourselves crying out simultaneously, "Thank you Lord" and "Give us more God, for we are not satisfied."

Robert Martin - Christian Missionary Alliance Pastor

I am a pastor in the Christian and Missionary Alliance and have a Ph.D. in New Testament Studies from Southwestern Baptist Theological Seminary. I mention the Ph.D. simply to emphasize that the experiences, which are recounted below, and other of my experiences of the last two years have been carefully thought through biblically, theologically, and historically. The work of the Holy Spirit in my life has been a developing, progressive experience with several specific crisis points. Gordon Fee, the respected Pentecostal New Testament scholar, has written a book entitled *God's Empowering Presence: The Holy Spirit in the Letters of Paul*. In speaking of the debate over whether there is an experience subsequent to conversion called "baptism in the Holy Spirit," Fee writes that "perhaps too much is made on both sides of single experiences. For Paul life in the Spirit begins at conversion; at the same time that experience is both dynamic and renewable" (Fee 1994, 864). Keeping the fact in mind that the work of the Holy Spirit in our lives is a continuing and dynamic process, let me briefly relate three significant experiences that I have had. Rather than trying to distinguish any one as my "baptism in the Holy Spirit" or my being "filled with the Spirit," I see each of them as examples of the continuing work of the Holy Spirit in my life.

In April of 1994 I went to Arlington, TX, to attend a conference on the Holy Spirit. Just preceding this conference was a meeting of Vineyard pastors in Plano, TX, which a friend and I also attended. Several of these pastors had recently been to the Toronto Airport Vineyard and had been touched by the Holy Spirit there.

I come out of a very traditional evangelical background and had never seen anything like the falling, laughing and shaking that I saw in these meetings. I quickly sensed, however, that God was somehow in this. I heard of lives drastically changed and I saw peace and joy in these people. Even though I was somewhat apprehensive, I finally went forward for prayer. As I was walking forward, I told the Lord that I hoped I wasn't being hard-hearted, but if I fell down it would have to be he that did it. As these Vineyard leaders began to pray for me, they prayed very quietly and they certainly were not trying to push me over because they did not even touch me. Suddenly, I felt a heat rising up my legs and I had to struggle just to stand up. I began to stumble around like a drunken man. The next thing I knew, I was lying on the floor. There was no great emotion as I lay there, but I had a great sense of peace. I also realized that my life would never be the same! In the next couple of days there was more prayer and I cried tears of repentance and brokenness. As I returned home, I could tell that something had happened and I knew that the Holy Spirit had touched me. As I prayed for people in my own church God began to touch them in a new way too.

In June of 1994 my family and I went to some meetings in Ft. Wayne, IN, where Randy Clark was speaking. I took my wife and two children and God also powerfully touched them. (I am writing this almost two years later and their lives have never been the same.) We got acquainted with Randy Clark in Ft. Wayne and in the next several months attended several other of his meetings in different places.

In November of 1994 we attended a series of meetings in Greensboro, NC. It was a Monday night meeting and we were still there at about 2:00 a.m. Only a few people remained. We prayed for the pastor of the Vineyard, Lee O'Hare, and he was powerfully touched by God and began to shake. My wife, Debbie, turned to me and said, "Let us pray for you." I had had almost no physical manifestations in the months since God started this new work in me. I think that she hoped something might happen to me so I would have a better understanding of those who did have these manifestations. It was so late and I was so tired that I just lay down on the carpet and told them to pray for me. As I lay there, my feet began to tingle and the thought came to me that someone should grasp my feet and pray for me. All of a sudden I felt someone grab my feet and I heard Randy Clark begin to pray. Then Randy moved up to my head and Lee went to my feet and they began to pray. My wife was on one side of me and a friend named Greg was on my other side. They were all praying for me. All of a sudden something hit me and I began to shake violently. Randy later said I looked like a frog being electrocuted. At the very moment that this power hit me, my wife and my friend Greg were knocked over backwards and began to laugh. After about twenty seconds the shaking stopped.

I had heard stories of people like D.L. Moody who had been powerfully touched by the Holy Spirit and they told the Lord to stay his hand because the experience was too intense. I had thought that if anything like that ever happened to me I would just say enlarge the vessel and I would tell the Lord to keep pouring it on. But after twenty seconds of this experience, I couldn't take any more. In fact, Randy started to pray for the Lord to send another wave and I started saying, "No, no, no." Some time later, I got up and I felt physically sick. (Somewhat like Daniel in Daniel 8:27 when he said he lay ill for several days after his encounter with the angel.) I walked about 100 feet and was so weak and felt so overwhelmed that I just lay down on the floor. I believe that this whole experience was God giving me a little glimpse of how awesome and powerful he really is.

The final experience I will mention was when Randy Clark was in Wilmore, KY, for a series of meetings. Jim Goll from Kansas City was speaking one morning. He was speaking about Peter walking on the water and how Peter brought Jesus back to those in the boat who were afraid to step out. I sensed a calling from God to help people come into a deeper experience of Christ. As I sat there, I began to weep. I don't cry like this very often and when I do it doesn't last long. But this time I just kept crying. They opened up the altar for people to come and pray and I went up and lay there and sobbed for more than two hours. Randy later commented to me that he had never seen me so emotional. God had touched something very deep in me. It seems the Lord was clarifying his call on my life and was breaking and humbling me to prepare me for what he had for me.

I could recount many more evidences of the Holy Spirit's work in my life over the last two years but I will stop here. These three experiences show that the Holy Spirit's work in our lives is a continuing one and will be expressed in the lives of different people in different ways. It may also be expressed in the same person in very different ways over the course of time. I want to close with the reminder that the greatest work of the Holy Spirit in our lives is to conform our characters to the image of Christ. The great aim of the Holy Spirit working in us is that we might be holy and that we might show forth in our lives in the purity, passion and power of our Lord.

Bob Balassi - Worship Leader St. Louis Vineyard

Bob is a successful computer analyst who works in the secular field. He is not prone to emotion, and is quite the analytical type. Yet, Bob's baptism in the Holy Spirit is one of the most inspiring stories I have heard. Here is his story:

Bob was sick with the stomach flu. Two of his five young children were also sick with the flu. Bob was hugging the commode when he heard his children beginning to throw up also. He said a short prayer about how God could heal his family. Suddenly his hands began to tingle, then to be electrified. He felt as if his fingers were going to blow off. Then he began to experience a gamut of emotions. He was laughing and then crying as he experienced the glory of God. Kathleen, his wife, came into the bathroom to observe her husband being baptized with the Holy Spirit. Bob had a profound sense of the majesty of God, his glory and splendor filled the bathroom, where Bob was overwhelmed. Praise and petitions filled his mouth. He left the bathroom to go pray for his children. Each was healed as well as Bob.

In this last chapter I wanted to give you some stories to encourage your faith and your hunger for a greater baptism in the Holy Spirit. These stories are not meant to show the only way that God does empower, but only a way that God can and does do it. If God can do it for many of these, then don't you think that He can do it for you? I want to encourage you to press in for more intimacy with God and more of His power for effective evangelism.

{References}

Basham, Don. 1969. *A Handbook on Holy Spirit Baptism*. Monroeville, Pennsylvania: Whitaker Books.

Bittlinger, Arnold. 1967. *Gifts and Graces—A Commentary on I Corinthians 12-14*. Grand Rapids, Michigan: William B. Eerdmans Publishing Company.

Bruner, Frederick Dale. 1970. *A Theology of the Holy Spirit*. Grand Rapids, Michigan: William B. Eerdmans Publishing Company.

Choy, Leona Fances. N.d. *Powerlines*. N.p.: Chariot Publishing (?).

Crawford, Mary. [1933] 1999. *The Shantung Revival*. Republication, St. Louis, Missouri: Global Awakening Publishing.

Culpepper, Robert H. 1977. *Evaluating the Charismatic Movement—A Theological and Biblical Appraisal*. Valley Forge, Pennsylvania: Judson Press.

Drummond, Lewis, ed. 1975. Reprint. *What the Bible Says—A Systematic Guide to Biblical Doctrines*. Nashville: Abingdon Press (page references are to reprint edition). Manufactured by Parthenon Press, Nashville, Tennessee. Original edition, N.p.: Marshall, Morgan, & Scott, 1974.

Dunn, James D.G. 1970. *Baptism in the Holy Spirit.*
London: SCM Press Ltd.

Ervin, Howard M. 1984. *Conversion-Initiation and the
Baptism in the Holy Spirit.* Peabody, Massachusetts:
Hendrickson Publishers, Inc.

Fee, Gordon D. 1991. *Gospel and Spirit—Issues in New
Testament Hermaneutics.* Peabody, Massachusetts:
Hendrickson Publishers, Inc.

----------. 1994. *God's Empowering Presence—The Holy
Spirit in the Letters of Paul.* Peabody, Massachusetts:
Hendrickson Publishers, Inc.

----------. 1996. *Paul, the Spirit, and the People of God.*
Peabody, Massachusetts: Hendrickson Publishers, Inc.

Finney, Charles G. 1978. *Revivals of Religion.* The
Christian Classics, 700 Club Edition. Virginia Beach,
Virginia: CBN University Press.

Graham, Billy. 1978. *The Holy Spirit—Activating God's
Power in Your Life.* Waco, Texas: Word Books
Publisher.

Grudem, Wayne. 1994. *Systematic Theology—An
Introduction to Biblical Doctrine.* Leicester, England:
Inter-Varsity Press; Grand Rapids, Michigan:
Zondervan Publishing House.

Hart, Larry. ~1975-6. *A Critique of American Pentecostal
Theology.* Ph.D. diss., Southern Baptist Theological
Seminary, Louisville, Kentucky.

Kendall, R.T. 1998. Reprint. *Understanding Theology—
The Means of Developing a Healthy Church in the
21st Century.* Geanies House, Fearn, Ross-shire, Great
Britain: Christian Focus Publications. Original edition,
Great Britain: Christian Focus Publications.

Lloyd-Jones, D. Martyn. 1984. *The Baptism and Gifts of
the Spirit.* Edited by Christopher Catherwood. Grand
Rapids, Michigan: Baker Books. Previously published
in England under the title Joy Unspeakable.

Lumpkin. W.L. [1959] revised 1969, reprint 1974 (page references are to reprint edition). *Baptist Confessions of Faith*. Valley Forge, Pennsylvania: Judson Press.

Menzies, William W. [1971] 1980. *Anointed to Serve*. Reprint, Springfield, Missouri: Gospel Publishing House.

Nathan, Rich, and Ken Wilson. 1995. *Empowered Evangelicals*. Ann Arbor, Michigan: Servant Publications, Vine Books.

Stott, John R. W. 1975. *Baptism & Fullness—The Work of the Holy Spirit Today*. Leicester England; Downers Grove, Illinois: Inter-Varsity Press. Previously published in England (1964) under the title The Baptism and Fullness of the Holy Spirit.

Stronstad, Roger. 1984. *The Charismatic Theology of St. Luke*. Peabody, Massachusetts: Hendrickson Publishers, Inc.

Suenens, Leon Joseph Cardinal. 1975. *A New Pentecost?* Translated by Francis Martin. New York: Seabury Press, Inc., A Crossroad Book.

Taylor, Jack R. 1983. *The Hallelujah Factor*. Nashville, Tennessee: Broadman Press.

Torrey, R. A. 1972. *The Baptism with the Holy Spirit*. Minneapolis: Bethany Fellowship, Inc., Dimension Books.

Tozer, A. W. N.d. *How to Be Filled with the Holy Spirit*. Camp Hill, Pennsylvania: Christian Publications, Inc.

Williams, J. Rodman. 1990. *Renewal Theology: Salvation, the Holy Spirit, and Christian Living*. Renewal Theology Series, vol. 2. Grand Rapids, Michigan: Zondervan Publishing House, Academic and Professional Books.

Note to reader:
This booklet employs the author-date system for text citations and references. This mode is highly recommended by the University of Chicago Press. Citations include the author's last name and the date of publication. Full bibliographical information is provided in the References list at the end of the booklet.

Other books by Randy Clark

Entertaining Angels

There Is More

Power, Holiness and Evangelism

Lighting Fires

God Can Use Little Ole Me

Other Booklets by Randy Clark

Evangelism Unleashed

Healing Ministry and Your Church

Learning to Minister Under the Anointing

Training Manuals Available

Ministry Team Training Manual

Schools of Healing and Impartation Workbooks

Core Message Series

Words of Knowledge

Biblical Basis of Healing

Baptism in the Holy Spirit

Open Heaven

Pressing In

The Thrill of Victory / The Agony of Defeat

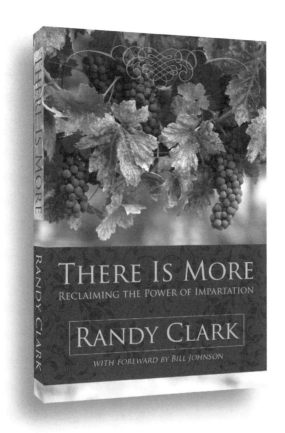

In "There Is More", Randy lays a solid biblical foundation for a theology of impartation as well as taking a historical look at impartation and visitation of the Lord in the Church. This is combined with many personal testimonies of people who have received an impartation throughout the world and what the lasting fruit has been in their lives. You are taken on journey throughout the world to see for yourself the lasting fruit that is taking place in the harvest field - particularly in Mozambique. This release of power is not only about phenomena of the Holy Spirit, it is about its ultimate effect on evangelism and missions. Your heart will be stirred for more as you read this book.

"This is the book that Randy Clark was born to write."

- Bill Johnson

GLOBAL SCHOOL OF SUPERNATURAL MINISTRY

Vision

To release followers of Christ into their specific destiny and calling, in order to live out the Great Commission.

Structure

Global School of Supernatural Ministry is a one or two year ministry school with an emphasis on impartation and equipping students for a life of walking in the supernatural. Classes start each September and end the following May. Courses are offered on-site at the Apostolic Resource Center in Mechanicsburg, PA. Upon completion of each program year a Certificate of Completion is awarded. Students seeking additional educational training may do so while attending GSSM through the Wagner Leadership Institute.

Community

The GSSM student body is diverse in age, culture, ministry experience, and educational accomplishments. From high school graduates to professionals to retirees - the students come together seeking more of God. Supernatural power, passion and honor are key values of GSSM and are reflected in our worship, outreach and personal relationships.

For more information - or to enroll in classes - contact us at
1-866-AWAKENING or apply online at
www.globalawakening.com/GSSM

globalawakening

For a schedule of upcoming events and conferences, or to purchase other products from Global Awakening, please visit our website at:

http://www.globalawakening.com